W. A. Bodell

The Spiritual Athlete and How he Trains

W. A. Bodell

The Spiritual Athlete and How he Trains

ISBN/EAN: 9783337428310

Printed in Europe, USA, Canada, Australia, Japan

Cover: Foto ©Lupo / pixelio.de

More available books at **www.hansebooks.com**

THE SPIRITUAL ATHLETE

AND

HOW HE TRAINS

BY

W. A. BODELL, A. B.

FLEMING H. REVELL COMPANY

NEW YORK   CHICAGO
30 Union Square, East   148–150 Madison St.

Publishers Evangelical Literature

INTRODUCTION.

I have been exceedingly interested in looking through the advance sheets of this little book.

The great need of the church and the world to-day is what has always been the need since the beginning—men of God. The spiritually strong man is born, not made. The source of his strength is his direct connection with the Source of all strength. He is not strong because he tries to be, but because he cannot help it. The secret of spiritual vigor and efficiency is in being in all things like unto Christ, who was able to say, 'My meat is to do the will of Him that sent me.'

I remember some years ago hearing a recent convert say that he had not understood what Paul meant when he said he "kept under his body." He did not comprehend how he could get under his body, but, he said, as he had grown in the knowledge of God, he had come to realize that what Paul meant was, that he kept his body under him.

The man whose thoughts and feelings and purposes are all born of God is the strong man, and the only man who ever is strong. For His workmen God has, as our brother says, prepared food; and he must have vigorous daily exercise. To neglect either will be to grow weak and worthless, or to perish. "The eyes of the Lord run to and fro throughout the whole earth to show Himself strong in behalf of them whose heart is perfect toward Him."

That the stirring words of our brother in this little treatise may have many readers, and that those who read may be led thereby into the secret of Him, who said, "Thy God hath commanded thy strength," is the sincere prayer of

His Friend,
B. FAY MILLS.

PREFACE.

To be strong physically is commendable, to be strong socially is desirable, to be strong intellectually is valuable, but to be strong spiritually is inestimable.

This little volume was not written for the gratification of the author but for the edification of the reader; if the reader by it be edified, then surely the author of it will be gratified.

The great need of Christians is not so much to know more as to do more. Not always those who know the most do the most; some know much and do little. Others know little and do much. This humble effort was intended that you should not only know more but that you might also do more. That coin which is not put into circulation is worthless; that talent which is not put to use is useless.

To see so many Christians who are educated and so few who are consecrated is lamentable; if they were no less educated but far more consecrated it would be far preferable. The cause of Christ needs no less education but more consecration. We do not need more strength so much as we need to use our strength more.

If we would become strong physically, we must obey the laws that will strengthen us physically; if we would become strong spiritually, we must obey the laws that will strengthen us spiritually. I have selected two of these which are most prominent and to which all others are subordinate; viz.: eating and exercising. If these laws are properly obeyed our spiritual strength will be greatly increased, if they are violated, they will be very much diminished.

Reader, this is the desire of the author— that you may be led spiritually to eat properly and exercise regularly—to study the word of the Lord and engage in the work of the Lord that you may grow strong in the Lord.

Yours in the Master's name,
                         W. A. BODELL.

THE SPIRITUAL ATHLETE

"HOW TO GET STRONG"

This is a question that many are asking. It is not, Have I sufficient strength? but, How can I get more? Few have more strength than they desire; none more than they need.

Of consecrated strength there is not enough; of desecrated strength there is too much. Strength used for good is blessed; strength used for evil is cursed. The one is used; the other is abused. The one is honorable; the other is dishonorable. The one has been used as it ought; the other has been used for naught. If we use our strength for the end intended, there can be no doubt but that our work will be rewarded.

What is the desire of our young men to-day? Is it not to get physical strength? They would rather be athletes physically, than be giants spiritually. You hear them talk more frequently about their muscle than about their mental caliber. The development of their bodies is to them of more importance than the development of their souls.

The care of the body is important, but the

care of the soul is urgent. To care more for your body than for your soul, is building for time; but to care more for your soul than for your body, is building for eternity.

Who is the hero amongst our young men? Is it the man who is always lagging behind, who goes moping along, whose tardiness is indicative of his laziness? No! It is the man that can jump the farthest, can run the fastest, can do the most daring feats; whose soul is buoyant, whose life is a pleasure, whose hope is an inspiration.

Who is it that our young men envy? Is it the man with puny body, bent form, slackened gait and sallow complexion? By no means! It is, after all, the man who looks the best, is the best, does the most, that they admire.

But it is not only so with the individual, it has been so with nations. Their games and combats, in which was displayed much physical strength, were a part of their religion. Greece had her heroes; she esteemed them gods. To the Grecians, to be victorious in the games was the greatest honor. Kings envied it; poets sang of it. To be victorious in war was much; to be conqueror in combat was more. Rulers were honored; victors were worshiped. Hercules, Theseus, Castor and Pollux were subduers of monsters. They slew lions, strangled serpents, overcame giants, were valiant in war, and were worshiped as gods. The Greeks had Ajax wrestling with Ulysses; Hercules with Achelous. To overcome in these, to the Greeks there was no higher honor. Who of them honored not Polydamas? They were more zealous for their physical beauty than for their moral integrity. They thought more of men's bodies than of their souls. They cared more for flesh than they did for spirit; more for the house than the one that lived in it.

Nor was Greece alone in this; other nations were like her. Rome had her games and tests of physical strength and endurance; no less than Greece did she esteem her strong men. These were her heroes. She had them enshrined in her temples as types of physical form and beauty.

GOD'S STRONG MEN

Nor have nations only valued physical strength; God himself has chosen strong men. Moses was a man of strength; else the flight into Midian would have exhausted him; the anxiety of the Exodus would have crushed him; the trials of the wilderness would have killed him; yet he withstood all, and when the Lord took him "his eyes were not dimmed, nor his natural force abated."

Elijah was a physical as well as a spiritual athlete. The eighteen-mile swift run in front of Ahab's chariot—how could he have accomplished it? the forty days' rapid flight through the desert—how could he have endured it? He was trained on the mountains; he was tried in the desert.

Saul was a strong man, of great stature—higher than any of the people, from his shoulders upward. But Saul prostituted his strength when like David he should have exclaimed, "My strength faileth because of mine iniquity." Though he at one time stood head-and-shoulders above his people, at another time he had sunken over head-and-shoulders into iniquity. His physical strength that crowned him was an awful contrast to the moral weakness which ruined him. Though he was a giant in physical strength without, he was too weak in spiritual strength to subdue the giant within.

Daniel was a man of strength, well-favored and without a blemish. He was worthy to stand before kings; but his moral strength was far greater than his physical strength. Paul was a man of great strength and physical endurance; though he had a thorn in the flesh he nevertheless had strength in his body; he accomplished much but he also endured much. "In labors he was more abundant, in stripes above measure, in prisons more frequent, in deaths oft. Of the Jews five times received he forty stripes save one. Thrice was he beaten with rods, once was he stoned, thrice he suffered shipwreck, a night and a day was he in the deep. In journeyings often, in perils of waters, in perils of robbers, in perils by his own countrymen, in perils by the heathen, in perils in the city, in perils in the wilderness, in perils in the sea, in perils among false brethren. In weariness and painfulness, in watchings often, in hunger and thirst, in fastings often, in cold and nakedness."

Oh, what a test of strength! What a fight he fought! What a race he ran! Who ever suffered as much without being exhausted? Who ever endured as much without being prostrated? But Paul was not more noted for his physical endurance than for his spiritual diligence. He was a trained athlete in the spiritual sphere; and the law of his life was, "Forgetting those things which are behind and reaching forth unto those things. which are before, I press toward the mark for the prize of the high calling of God in Jesus Christ."

THE STRENGTH OF THE BODY

Who would disparage the importance of physical strength? The body is the .instrument of the will. We usually will what we do, but we do not always what we will. Sometimes we will more than we are able to do. The body often forsakes what the will undertakes. The rapacity of the will is often more than the capacity of the body. Our wills often attempt what our bodies prevent. Where is the profit in having a strong will and a weak body?

Napoleon had an indomitable will but he had also enduring strength; he had a will that dared much but he also had a body that endured much. Had his body been inefficient, then his will would have been more than sufficient. To have more strength than you have will is useless; to have more will than you have strength is weakness. Many have desired to do good who have not been able; many have been able to do good who have not desired it. Who would be weaker than is necessary? Who would not rather have strength to accomplish what they desired, than desire what they are not able to accomplish? To have a tenacity of purpose and no purpose of tenacity is useless; to have one and not the other is fruitless; to have both is to accomplish whatsoever we desire; but let us be careful that we desire only what is right to accomplish.

Let us get strength and for good use it; rather than having it and for evil lose it.

THE STRENGTH OF THE SOUL

But however important physical strength may be spiritual strength is more important.

"Exercise thyself rather unto godliness. For exercise profiteth a little; but godliness is profitable unto all things, having the promise of the life that now is, and of that which is to come."

"But know ye not that your bodies are the temples of the Holy Ghost?"

To care more for your body than for your soul would be like taking care of the altar and letting the fire go out that is to burn thereon. Who would throw away the sword and keep the scabbard? Who would throw away the jewel and keep the casket? To neglect our souls for the sake of our bodies would be throwing away the gold and keeping the dross. Our souls are as far more important than our bodies as eternity is longer than time, or as heaven is higher than the earth. There is a natural and there is a spiritual body; the first is of the earth earthy, the second is from heaven heavenly. Our bodies are temporal but our spirits are eternal. Our body shall return to dust and ashes, but our spirits unto God who gave them.

You may destroy the body, but you cannot destroy the soul.

I would not discourage you in getting physical strength, but I would encourage you in getting spiritual strength. If the one is valuable, then the other is inestimable.

"Thou shalt need all the strength that God can give,
  Simply to live, my friend, simply to live."

"For we wrestle not against flesh or blood, but against principalities, against powers, against spiritual wickedness in high places." Spiritual foes cannot be overcome by carnal weapons; spiritual giants cannot be overcome by physical strength. David could slay the giant of the Philistines with a sling and a stone, but he could not overcome the giant within him, with all the power at a king's command. If we want to overcome our spiritual enemy, Satan, we must use spiritual weapons. Take the sword of the spirit, which is the word of God; with it the Saviour foiled the Devil. "It is written, It is written," is worth more than a Damascus blade; "And thus saith the Lord," more than a swift-flying arrow. Wherefore take the whole armor of God. Notice we are to take it, not to make it. Our king furnishes it, and we must use it; but if we are to use it, we must have strength to wield it. Either Saul's armor was too much for David, or David was not enough for Saul's armor. He could not fight Goliath with that; so he put it away from him.

Oh, that there were multitudes of men spiritually strong, that they might take the whole armor of God and wield it! Oh, for strength—spiritual strength—that we might slay spiritual giants, be valiant in battle and overcome our spiritual enemy!

"Be strong, be strong!" that is the admonition; to him that overcometh is the reward. But how shall we overcome when we are spiritually undone? Unless we conquer Satan he will conquer us. We shall never conquer him unless we have strength to overcome him.

THE WAY OF STRENGTH

But how shall we get strength?

How do we get strong, physically? **By** believing in some theory of physical culture? By having faith in some system of gymnastics? Will that give us strength? Whoever developed muscle by simply believing that there was a way by which it was done? No one. Nor can we; it is impossible. Yet some think they can obtain spiritual strength after this fashion. There are only two ways in which it can be obtained:

1. BY EATING.

2. BY EXERCISING.

These are the conditions of gaining physical strength; they are also the conditions of gaining spiritual strength. If it is impossible to gain physical strength by a theory then it is impossible to gain spiritual strength without practice. It may thus be desired but it cannot thus be acquired. The same law that rules in the physical sphere also rules in the spiritual sphere. There are two principal conditions in gaining physical strength; there are also but two in obtaining spiritual strength; viz: Eating properly and exercising properly.

SPIRITUAL FOOD

First, then, we must eat. Jeremiah declares that "The words of the Lord were found and he did eat them." The Lord said to Ezekiel, "Son of man, eat this roll." What did he mean? Literally that he should eat the roll? Yes, he was to feed upon it spiritually as men feed upon food physically. He was to read it, study it, believe it; just as with food, we are to eat it, masticate it, assimilate it. As we convert what we eat into physical muscle by known physical laws, so we are to convert what we read into moral muscle by similar spiritual laws.

But instead of feeding upon the word many are destroying it. There are two ways of treating seed. The naturalist cuts it up and discourses upon it; the husbandman reaps it and feeds upon it. The one may ascertain the characteristics of it, but the other derives strength from it. Similarly men are treating the gospel. The critic dissects it, raises a mountain of doubt about it, but does not receive any strength from it; the simple-minded husbandman sows it, reaps it, and lives upon it.

So we are to feed upon the word. What would be the result physically if we stopped eating? We would soon die. But what is the result spiritually of those of us who stopped reading? Many of us are dead.

I fear of many it might be said as was said of the church in Sardis, "Thou hast a name that thou livest, and art dead."

Many of us have starved our souls. Our souls can no more live upon nothing than our bodies. It is by eating that we sustain life. When we stop eating we stop living. Where there is life, there is growth; when we stop living, we stop growing. A tree that has no life has no growth. Where there is growth, there is strength; that which has no growth has no strength. Where growth ends, strength declines; where it continues, it remains. Would we have strength? Then we must have life. Would we have life? Then we must do that which sustains life—we must eat.

HOW TO EAT

So we must do spiritually; our spiritual natures must be fed. There is a natural and there is a spiritual body; we care for the natural, but shall we starve the spiritual? We are careful of the less, but do not care much for the greater. If our bodies have no nutriment they will soon suffer detriment. If our spiritual bodies fast long they will not last long. Our spiritual bodies are not to be fed upon natural food, any more than our natural bodies are to be fed upon spiritual food. The natural is from below, but the spiritual is from above. Shall we feed that which is from above by that which comes from below? The one is to be fed on natural food, the other on spiritual food. But how shall we eat spiritual food? Very much in the same way that we eat physical food; the one goes into our mouths, the other into our minds. As we masticate physical food with our mouths, so we absorb spiritual food with our minds. Eating is reading; digesting is studying; assimilating is believing. The physical food that goes through this process becomes physical strength; the spiritual food that goes through a similar process becomes spiritual strength. The food that we eat has become a part of us, after we have assimilated it; so the matter that we read has become a part of us, after we have believed it. If we want to feed upon the word of God, let us read it, study it, believe it, then it will become a part of our spiritual body, as the food we eat by a similar process becomes a part of our natural

bodies.   But what shall we say of those who
never eat spiritually?   Never eat anything
that will strengthen their spiritual bodies?
They are skeletons! hideous, frightful!   Oh,
that we could only see ourselves spiritually
as we see ourselves physically.   What hideous things we would behold!

I shall never forget the impression made
upon me, when, a few years ago, I saw a
man who had determined to starve himself;
he had concluded that it was all foolishness
to eat, so he determined to eat no more. When
I saw him he had taken no food for several
weeks; and what a sight!   A living man with
a body like that of the dead; pale, emaciated;
eyes sunken, cheeks fallen, beauty of form gone,
his body a skeleton, his limbs like sticks, his
fingers like claws.   Could the graves give up
their dead, none more horrible could come
forth.   It was a deathly picture of a living
being!   But, my reader, could we but behold
our spiritual body we might see as terrible
a spectacle as this.   Because we can not see
our spirit and do not realize its condition we
think it is not so bad.   But unless our spirit
feeds carefully, it will look as terribly.

WHAT TO EAT

Much also depends upon *what* we eat; eating nothing is bad, but eating everything is little better. If we eat nothing we will soon be famishing. If we eat everything we will soon be perishing. If we do not eat carefully we must suffer accordingly There is some food which will strengthen us, but there is also food which will weaken us. Eating food which is substantial, is doing that which is essential. Animals eat by intuition; we eat according to fruition. Animals seldom eat what is not meet; we often eat what we do not need.

Thus it is physically, but how is it spiritually? As much depends upon what we eat, so much depends upon what we read. If by eating improperly we can ruin our bodies, so by reading improperly we may ruin our souls. Care in eating is not more important than care in reading. Upon what, then, have we been living spiritually? Have we been living upon strengthening meats or upon softening sweets?

It is not very difficult to tell upon what some men feed. Whatever our nature craves, that is upon what we generally live. Few eat what they would not; many eat what they

should not.   Some of our appetites are depraved, and we often feed upon what we
should not have.   When we only eat what
we would, and cannot eat what we should,
then, alas, what is our condition?   We are to
know men by their fruits, but more often we
can judge them better by their pursuits.   What
we desire often shows the brand of us better
than what we require.   We do not always
have the greatest greed for that which is our
greatest need. If we have an appetite for
sweets, we seldom live on meats.

FEEDING ON ASHES

Look at some of our young men!   Upon
what do they feed their spiritual bodies?
Their countenance speaks it, their conversation reveals it, their associations tell it, their
life confirms it: "They feed on ashes."   Some
of our young men, who go about our cities
without a fiber of Christian strength, with
more collar than conscience, more cane than
character, more starch than "stuff"—it is not
difficult to tell upon what they live.   It is
this miserable saloon, billiard-hall, gambling-
den, street and alley bill of fare.   It comes
up from the pit.   It smites and blasts and de-
stroys whoever partakes of it.   Like salt at

the roots of a tree, it will kill it. There is no spiritual strength derived from these for our spiritual nature, unless our spirits are of a very vicious nature. Satan's food will be for Satan's good; he who feeds upon it will sooner or later suffer from it.

THE WORD A TABLE

But you say, Where shall we get spiritual food? If we would get strong in the Lord we must feed upon His word. The Lord has given us our spirits, and He has not left us without food for them. Read the word, study it, believe it. It is a table prepared by our Master; loaded with good things for our spiritual bodies. How many might partake of it, who, alas, never taste of it. But for what we have no desire, that we think we do not require. Medicine is often bitter to us, but nevertheless it is necessary for us.

But why do we not eat that which is good, that our souls may delight in fatness? If we fed upon the word of God, we would never be found in spiritual weakness. But, you say, I would read the Bible more if it were not so tedious. But is it not because you are irreligious? If we always feed upon that only which is agreeable, we will at last be found wanting, and be eternally miserable. Simply to eat what we crave is often to feed the depraved nature that we have. To read only what we like, often tells that we like what we ought not to read. If we say that we cannot feed upon the word, then our taste has been very much perverted; and the only remedy for such perversion is a genuine conversion. To read simply to gratify our taste, may, instead of strengthening us, spiritually ruin us. We may have the appearance of life, but, like a tree smitten with the blight, there is the presence of death.

The reading of healthy books is good, but the reading of the Book of books is far better. I would not say that we should read the former less, but I would say read the latter more. How many give other advice! They say, Read everything. That would be as disastrous as to eat everything. They will tell us that the Bible is a dead book, because they get no life from it; that it has no strength in it, because they derive no strength from it. They would have us believe that if we desire to be wise we must read everything. That is the voice of Satan; it is the same story that he told in Eden. It is the same lie that he had Adam and Eve believe. The Lord told them not to eat of the fruit of the garden, but Satan persuaded them that the Lord was mistaken, and that if they ate of all the fruit of the garden, they would be as gods, knowing good from evil. They ate and their eyes were opened; but oh! what a sad revelation it must have been! True, now they began to know good from evil, but hitherto they had known no evil. But from hence, alas, they began to know less of good than they did of evil. And now ye who tempt us to read that which is not good, are you not like Satan? The fruit that you are trying to have us eat, is it not forbidden? You tell us that there is nothing gained in reading the Bible, read something that will give large ideas; get a knowledge of the world; read something that will give an idea of the other side of life. What if we follow your advice? What a sad experience we will have. Instead of becoming as gods, we will more likely become as devils. Before we had known no evil, therefore we did that which was good; now we know but little good, therefore we do that which is evil. Better to have no experience than to have a sad experience; better not see than to see only that which is evil; better know nothing at all than to know only that which will cause us to fall.

He who knows nothing but good is sometimes called a fanatic; but he who knows nothing but evil ought to be regarded as satanic. To see nothing but good may be short-sightedness; but to see nothing but evil ought to be regarded as terrible wickedness. To know both and do that which is right is good enough; but to know both and do that which is wrong is bad enough.

HOW TO HEAL DISEASES

Now there is something in that Book of books for every weakness. There is no spiritual disease but that there is a prescription for it. There is no spiritual ailment but what there is a remedy for it. Physicians prescribe different diets for different diseases; so in this book there are special portions for special difficulties. If we are following afar off, read the abiding chapter (John 15); if we have backslidden, read the backslider's chapter (Jer. 3); if we are hungry, read the bread chapter (John 6); if we have no moral strength, read the character chapter (Job 29); if we are halting, read the come chapter (Isa. 55); if we are being overcome, read the conquerors' chapter (Luke 4); if we are enslaved, read the deliverance chapter (Psa. 18); if we are unbelieving, read the faith chapter (Heb. 11); if we are thirsty, read the living water chapter (John 4); if we are weary, read the rest chapter (Heb. 4); if we are wandering, read the refuge chapter (Psa. 46); if we are weak, read the tonic chapter (Psa. 27); if we are lazy, read the work chapter (Jas. 2).

There are as many diseases of the soul as there are of the body; but there are also as many remedies for the diseases of the soul as there are remedies for the diseases of the body. Drunkenness is a spiritual dropsy, but Prov. 20:1, with Cor. 12:9, ought to be a sufficient remedy. Self-confidence is a spiritual lethargy, but 1 Cor. 10:12, and Matt. 26:41, ought to wake us from such vanity. Envy is a spiritual canker, but Matt. 5:29 to 30, ought to do away with the "blear-eyed monster." Lust is a spiritual fever; Gal. 5-6, ought to check it forever. Backsliding is a spiritual relapse, but Jeremiah 2:19 and 3:12 to 13, ought to restore us to our former state. Hardness of heart is a spiritual stone, but Jeremiah 23:29, ought to break it to pieces. A seared conscience is a spiritual apoplexy; Hebrews 9:14, ought to arouse it to great activity. Pride is a spiritual tumor, but Proverbs 16:18, ought to awaken us to its danger.

Be sure we read just what we need; to read what we ought not to read is as disastrous spiritually, as to eat what we ought not to eat physically. If we knew the consequences of eating carelessly, then we would take heed to the consequences of reading foolishly. Could we but see the consequences spiritually as we see them physically, then would we still be so foolish? If we but saw the consequences physically would we still be so careless? Are we to eat indigestible food for poor digestion? Then are we to recommend the hardest portions of the word for a weak Christian?

There is something in knowing what to eat; then is there nothing in knowing what to read? In the former, ignorance is dangerous, but in the latter it is perilous. I know a young man who said he was a Christian until he began to read the Bible. "Well," I asked him, "how much do you read it?" He replied, "I read it every day." "But how do you read it?" "Why, in the evening before I retire I take my Bible, and where I happen to open, there I read." How ridiculous! Whoever would think of eating in this way?

What do you think of that man, who, having tramped the streets for several days in a vain effort to get something to eat, passes a grocery, and being desperate, he says to himself, "I must have something to eat, and I will step into that grocery and the first thing I see I will eat." He steps into the grocery, and the first thing he sees is a long bar of soap; but he must keep his word, so he takes that soap and eats it.

Do you think that appeased his hunger any? I do not know which would be the worst, to die for something to eat or to eat something from which men are sure to die. Oh, you say, that is ridiculous! Yes, but reading the Bible just where we happen to open might be just as disastrous. Soap is useful in its place. It is good for cleansing, but who would think of appropriating it for eating? Bread is good for eating, but who would think of using it for washing? The one is just as absurd as the other; both were in that grocery; if he had used discretion he would have gone a step farther and taken the bread. Both are in the Bible; there are portions for cleansing, and portions for eating; but the man who says, "I will read just where I open," may have to read that with which he should have cleansed himself.

A COMMON ERROR

If we would feed with as much care spiritually as animals feed physically, then it would be much better.   When I was a boy I used to feed my father's flock, in the evening I would give them fodder and hay.   The next morning when I would go to feed them again I would find that they had eaten all the good part of the fodder and had eaten out all the good hay, but there were the briers and the hard stalks; you could not make them eat that.   Do we eat with as much discretion?   No!   And alas, what a sad confession.   We pick out all the good hay, tear off all the good leaves and husks from the fodder and throw them away and then try to eat the briers and stalks.   That is the way, alas, that many of us read the Bible. We hunt out all the difficult portions, pick out all the good that is in them, throw them away and try to eat what remains.

Oh, that we read the word as God intended it, then there would be no need of the men who have so ably defended it.   When read aright, there is nothing better; when read all wrong there is nothing worse.   Would we read it all right?   Read it then by the aid of the spirit. Should we read it all wrong, it will not be long until we will deny it. If we read it carefully, it will get us wisdom; if we read it prayerfully it will get us salvation.

THE WAY OF WEAKNESS

How much do we read our Bibles? Do we read them three times a day? If we do not, then we are not spiritual. If we do not read them at all, then our condition is critical. To care more for our bodies than for our souls is to be eternally miserable; to care more for our souls than for our bodies is infinitely preferable. Oh, that men would look after the things that are eternal and not so much after the things temporal. I knew a young man, who was the pride of a father's home and the joy of a mother's heart. But he decided to leave his home and go into the city; against his mother's requests and his father's protests he decided to go. As he was getting ready his mother brought him his Bible and put it in his trunk. It was a sad day when he left his father's house and broke his mother's heart. When he came to the city he immediately went to the place where he expected to be employed. His expectations were realized; he at once began to work as best he could; that day was lonesome for him, he seemed lost; no one cared for him.   The next morning he went to his place of business with a heavy heart.   The other clerks notice it, and they say to one another, "Do you see that greenhorn from the country?   We will have to take him out and show him the sights."   So they come up to him and say, "Won't you go out with us to-night and have a time?   We will show you the city."   "No," said he, "I cannot go; I must find a lodging place and unpack my trunk."   "O pshaw! what is the matter with you? Are you one of those 'goody goody' fellows?   I suppose you read your Bible three times a day; but you will soon get over that.   Come on!   You might just as well be broken in now as any time; you will be broken in sooner or later anyway."   But he said, "No, I do not care to go to-night."

That evening he went out looking for a lodging place; he soon found one; he sent to the depot for his trunk; he took it to his room, began to unpack it, and when he came to his Bible he remembered what the clerks at the store had said, and he thought, "I will not need that," and he put it down in the bottom of his trunk.   There it remained for six months. Meanwhile he was getting weak morally. He began to engage in the unholy conversation of the clerks, enjoy their smutty stories, laugh at their dirty jokes. He gradually, though perhaps unconsciously, was forsaking his Saviour and taking sides with Satan. His associates were aware of it and rejoiced in it, so they said to him, "Do you still read your Bible?" "No," he replied, "I have given that up; there is nothing in doing it." "Well," they say, "you are ready to go out with us now are you not?" "Yes," said he, "I will be glad to go."

THE FATAL STEP

Out into the paths of sin they went. Oh! I think every angel of darkness smiled as from one place to another they went. At the door of places of enchantment he halted as if the voice of his mother was saying to him, "My son, come not nigh to that door; it is the way to hell, going down to the chambers of death." But his comrades say, "Come on!" "Come on!" And in he goes, "straightway as the ox to the slaughter, or as a fool to the correction of the stocks; and he knoweth not that it is for his life." Oh, the awful work was done! He had purchased a through ticket, on a lightning-express train, on a down-grade, broad gauge, to perdition. What was the fatal step in this young man's life? When he left home? No! When he engaged in the ungodliness of his associates? No! When he said that he would go out with them? No! When he went? No! When he stood at the door of enchantment, debating whether he should go in and then went? No! It was when he forsook his Bible and put it down in the bottom of his trunk. He threw away his pass to heaven and got a through-pass to hell.

Oh, what, with the wine-cup and the gambler's dice and the scarlet enchantress, is the young man to do without the grace of God in his heart and moral fiber in his soul?

BUT WHY?

But why did he not have this muscle and fiber? Simply because he did nothing that would give it to him; he ate no spiritual food; he had no spiritual strength. The dirty jokes, the smutty stories of his fellows could not be nourishing to his moral and spiritual nature. Neither did he get much nourishment out of his Bible down in the bottom of his trunk. Ah! there was the trouble! Who would think of living six months on a lunch kept in the bottom of a trunk? No one; you would have to eat it, if you wanted to get any strength from it. That was the trouble with this young man; he never read his Bible; it did not become daily food for him.

Say, my reader, how often do we read our Bible? Can we say as Job did, "I have esteemed the word of His mouth more than necessary food?" Is it our daily food? Has it become meat and drink for our souls? If it has not, spiritually are we not getting very weak? Have we ever had any spiritual life, or are we spiritually dead? "Verily I say unto you ye must be born again." Have we once lived and now are dead? Then there must be another resurrection. The Saviour must again cry, with a loud voice, "Lazarus, come forth!"

I once heard a man say that he could not see how some people lived spiritually unless they lived like a tape-worm—upon what someone else ate. A homely illustration, but, alas, how true! Some of us never eat for ourselves. We expect someone else to prepare our food for us. Yes, and spiritually we often expect them to eat it for us. We expect others to read for us, study for us, and then give the fruit of it to us. This cannot be done, any more than others can eat for us, masticate for us or digest for us. If good, substantial meat of the word is too much for us then we had better feed upon the milk awhile; at all events it would be better than to have someone else eat for us. Many of us expect the minister to prepare our spiritual food for us, and feed us, like a child, once a week. When others prepare our food for us they season it according to their own tastes. I fear it is so with our spiritual food, when others prepare it; they prepare it to suit their own tastes; they season it with their own ideas— the opinions of men, with the philosophies of their own liking, with the wisdom of the world. We must have a stout digestion to feed on some men's theology; no sap, no spring, no life, but all stern accuracy, without any spiritual fervency, it is a cold meal indeed.

To turn stones into bread was a temptation of our Master, but alas! how many yield to a worse temptation, to turn bread into stone.

Let us have the pure milk and meat of the word. Spices are good enough for the palate but they will not give fiber to the soul. Seasoning may be desirable but it will not be profitable. People are often taken more with the seasoning than with the word itself; they have come to like spices very much. Feed upon the good meat yourself and do not eat the pudding that someone else has made out of it. It may taste well to you, but it will not be well for you.

IMPROPER FOOD

Then again those who prepare our food for us are often so accommodating that they will not consider what is best for us, but prepare our food to suit our own tastes, no matter what that may be. How many are there whose health has been ruined in this way? But, alas! how many are there whose souls have been ruined in a similar way? Instead of feeding us on good spiritual truth they feed us on what we want and not what we need. I once knew an experienced cook of a private club who prepared for them just what they wanted. When the health of a few had given way, the physician instructed him not to do so again, and asked him why he did it. "Well," said he, "if I did not, I would have lost my position long ago." Does not that explain why

so many feed their flock upon what they want
and not upon what they need?

HOW TO EAT

Then much depends upon *how* we eat.
We must eat regularly. If we ate three or
four meals one day and then omitted three or
• four days, what do you think would be the
consequences? How do you think we would
fare if we were to eat one big meal on Sunday and then not eat anything for a whole
week? But who would think of eating in that
way? No one; but spiritually how many eat
more irregularly than that. There are some
who think they can read enough of the word
on Sunday to last them during all the week
days. We might just as well try to eat
enough on Sundays to last all week. Some
of us do not even that; we must be fed on
Sundays and that is all the spiritual food we
get. There are some of us who read a chapter on New Year's day and then we will read
no more until the next New Year's day. We
are like the man who always read the 103
Psalm on Thanksgiving day, and that was all
that he read the whole year. Now what
would you think of the man who would eat
one big meal on Thanksgiving day and then

would eat nothing more until the next Thanksgiving day? Physically it is impossible, but spiritually we think it probable. If the one is not reasonable then the other cannot be profitable. If we were to do so physically we would soon have dyspepsia; if we attempt the latter we will soon have a bad case of spiritual mania. There are a great many spiritual dyspeptics who have eaten so irregularly that their spiritual stomachs are out of order. They cannot digest even the simplest kind of food; nothing will stay down. This is why so many go to church on Sundays, hear a good sermon and then go out and throw it all off. It gives them no strength; it is no source of help to them. Unless a man feeds regularly on spiritual food on week-days, he will not get much good out of what he eats on Sundays. How would we fare if we did not eat anything during the week-days and then ate a big meal on Sundays? Would we fare very well? No, we would fare very ill. There are many who try to feed that way spiritually, and then what they hear on Sundays lies on them heavily. If we eat foolishly we must suffer physically; if we read irregularly we must suffer spiritually. If you feed well you will feel well; if you read well you will fare well.

"THREE MEALS A DAY"

How many meals do we eat a day? Do any of us eat but one? No, most of us eat three and then some of us are hungry. But how often do we sit down to that feast, the Bible, and eat a good meal? Do we do it three times a day? If not, then we care more for our physical nature than for our spiritual nature. In this age we have not much time to think about spiritual things that shall last throughout eternity, but are altogether absorbed with temporal things which will end with time. We must look after the things that are temporal and let go of the things that are eternal. We have not time to feed upon the word which will strengthen us, but like busy men we seize a small portion and swallow it and leave it to trouble us. We never take time to masticate it, digest it, assimilate it— to read it, study it, believe it. As men become miserably affected physically, so we become seriously dejected spiritually. Oh, that we were as fearful of spiritual perdition as we are careful of our physical condition. If our souls are of more value than our bodies why then should we starve them? If we treated our bodies as we do our souls, we should not long have them. Would we then be strong spiritually, then let us feed upon the word regularly. If we starve our body we abuse it; if we starve our soul we will lose it. If we were to eat one meal a year our bodies would soon be famishing; if we read the word but once a year, our souls will soon be perishing. Salvation comes by believing, but how can there be firm believing without much spiritual reading? Spiritually, he that reads much, will also believe much. Constant reading gives firm believing. A prayerful reader makes a strong believer. If we would only read more, then we would believe more.

LIVING ON THE PAST

I fear too many of us are living too much upon things of the past and not enough upon the things of the present. We are after all like ruminating animals; we chew the cud; we eat again and again what we have eaten before. We are like the man who had a wonderful experience when he was converted. It was a great feast for him. He tried to live upon his experience. He used to repeat it over and over and get much comfort out of it. When he would get despondent, he would repeat his experience and meditate upon it, and he would get much consolation from it.

When his faith failed him he would fall back upon his experience.   Finally he became old and feeble and he was afraid of forgetting his experience.   So he wrote it out, and carefully put it away with his deeds of land to keep until the time of need.   When the time came for him to die he felt very much the need of something to comfort him in that trying hour. He sent his grandson to bring him his experience; he went and returned with the sad news that the rats had eaten up his experience and made a nest of it.   Alas!   All his hope was gone!   He must die in despair! He had nothing left to cling to;   that upon which he had been depending all his lifetime, and what he thought was a title-deed to everlasting life, was gone.   He had had a glorious experience, but he died a hopeless death.   What was the matter? Why, instead of living upon the word and growing thereby, he tried to live upon an old experience, and starved thereby.

I have a bill of fare of a rich repast of which I partook years ago.   How do you think I would have fared, if, instead of eating daily,   I would have gotten that old bill of fare and looked over it and thought of the good things I had to eat then?   Do you think I would have become strong and healthful?

No! I would be weak and pitiful. That is just what this man tried to do; he was dead spiritually long before he was dead physically. Instead of living upon daily food as we ought to do, he tried to live upon the experience which he had forty years ago. But how many of us are trying to live in the same way? Instead of feeding upon the word, we are thinking of an experience that we once had, and expect to live upon it. I might just as well expect to live upon that old bill of fare physically as to expect to live upon an experience that I have had spiritually. There are many who can tell us a grand experience; but that is usually all they can tell us. They will tell you that they have been Christians "Lo, these many years." They can tell you the exact day and hour when they had that experience, but that is as far as they ever get. They depend more upon thinking about their old experience than they do upon studying the word. Many of them may not die experienceless, yet they may die Christless. When we are born, we might just as well ever after expect to live without eating, as when we are converted, ever after expect to live without reading. The one would cause physical death; the other would cause spiritual

death.   We might just as well depend upon
a meal that we ate forty years ago, as to attempt to live upon an experience we had forty
years ago.   None are foolish enough to
attempt the former, but how many are in-
cautious enough and do attempt the latter.
The one is foolishness, the other is carelessness, but both would be hopeless.

BE TEMPERATE

Then again we should not eat too much.
We may eat too much, but can we read too
much?   There is just as much danger of reading too much as there is of eating too much.
As we may eat too much, however substantial
the food may be, so may we read too much,
however good the matter may be.   It is more
serious to overload our minds than to overload our stomachs.   Our minds suffer from
the transgression of spiritual laws; our bodies
suffer from the transgression of physical laws.
The laws which govern our physical bodies
are wonderful, but the laws which govern our
spiritual bodies are fearful.   How often have
we heard this question asked: "Can we read
the Bible too much?"   Why not? Can we not
overload our minds as well as our stomachs?
The one operates physically, the other operates

spiritually; both are governed by laws. When we transgress these laws our bodies and minds must suffer for it. A hospital is bad enough, but an insane asylum is far worse. Hospitals are prisons for the transgression of physical laws; insane asylums are prisons for the transgression of spiritual laws; penitentiaries are prisons for the transgression of civil laws. If we transgress we must pay the penalty for that transgression. The higher the law the greater the penalty for its transgression. If then the spiritual laws are the highest, are not the penalties for their transgression the greatest? If the penalty for physical transgression is twofold then the penalty for spiritual transgression must be one hundredfold. If by eating too much we suffer temporal pain, then by reading too much we may suffer eternal woes. As our bodies are temporal their pains must be temporal; but as our spirits are eternal, their woes must be eternal. The punishment hereafter for the sins of this life will not be physical, but spiritual. We suffer the punishment of physical transgression in time, but we suffer the punishment of spiritual transgression in eternity.

PUNISHMENT—TEMPORAL AND ETERNAL

Shall the sin which is committed temporally be punished eternally? Our bodies are temporal, therefore their punishment will be temporal; but our souls are eternal, and shall their punishment not be eternal? Men say, "Can a crime which is committed temporally be punished eternally?" If that crime is a transgression of temporal laws it will be temporal; if it is a transgression of eternal laws, then it will be eternal. Murder is a transgression of both temporal and eternal laws, therefore its punishment will be both temporal and eternal. So it is with overeating and overreading. The former transgression is temporal, its punishment will be temporal; the latter transgression is eternal, therefore its punishment will be eternal. Oh! if the suffering of physical wrecks is such that, though alive, they wish themselves dead, what must be the suffering of spiritual wrecks, who, being dead, wish themselves alive? To be alive, with physical pain, is still far better than to be physically dead, with eternal pain.

Have not men been ruined spiritually by reading the Bible too much? Many have overloaded their spiritual stomachs and have become set against spiritual food. We may be turned against spiritual food by reading too much, in the same way that we may be turned against physical food by eating too much.

I know of an instance where a man determined to read the Bible through three times a year. He did it the first year; the second year he read it through once, now he does not read it at all, but has become very skeptical. What was the cause of all this? Was it the reading of the Bible? No! It was the improper reading of it. Instead of taking proper food from it daily, and digesting it thoroughly—that is, studying it—he kept overloading his stomach until he wrecked his spiritual digestion and lost his appetite. He blamed the food instead of his improper eating of it. If a man should eat ten big meals a day and then become dyspeptic shall he blame the food for it? If a man overloads himself with spiritual food and becomes a skeptic shall he then blame the Bible for it? Not at all!

OVER-MUCH READING A FOLLY

To determine to read the Bible through three times a year may be just as foolish a determination as to determine to see how much you can possibly eat for a whole year. If he attempted the latter he would soon be dead physically; if he attempts the former he will soon be dead spiritually. What is the matter with a great many of our Christians who read the Bible a good deal, and yet go about with long faces and sad countenances, as though they expected to live but a short time? The truth is, spiritually they are already dead; they have overeaten. "And they are of all men most miserable." Better not eat enough and digest it, than to eat too much and regret it. So we had better not read enough and study it than to read too much and afterward lament it. Good food is a blessing when properly eaten, but it will be a curse if improperly eaten. So the Bible is a blessing when rightly read, but it may become a curse when foolishly read. Oh! that we knew how, and what to read! Eat what is meet; read what we need.

NO APPETITE

But, you say, I have no appetite for spiritual food. But why should it be anything astonishing that we do not like food which is spiritually nourishing? Unless we are spiritually minded, spiritual food will not greatly be desired; unless we get thirsty for the living waters we will not drink at the flowing fountain. The word is not much of a tonic for a spiritual disease which is chronic. Sin is not much of a stimulant to spiritual nourishment. Ever since our first parents ate the fruit which was forbidden, we have a special desire to eat the fruit which they have eaten. But we must learn to eat spiritual food. The food that we at first relish the least, is often what we afterward enjoy the most. Food that we used to crave, is what we ought not now to have. To eat the food which is not for our spiritual strengthening, will be to feed upon food that will be to us spiritually weakening. So, often we eat only what we like, but, alas! we often like what we ought not to eat. If we would like spiritual meat then we must learn to eat it; if we do not learn to eat it, then by and by we will come to hate it.

EXERCISE AND APPETITE

But there is another way by which we can obtain an appetite: by exercising.

"Be ye doers of the word and not hearers only." We who serve the Lord have an appetite for his word. If we have no appetite for his word, it is evident that we have not desired to serve the Lord. Proper exercise will give us a good appetite. We who are

good workers usually are good eaters.   If
we exercise properly, we will eat heartily. If
physical exercise will give us good physical
appetites, then will not spiritual exercise give
us good spiritual appetites?   Work for the
Lord will give us a desire for his word, and
if we serve the Lord continually we will love
his word heartily.   To love and not to serve
is hypocrisy; to serve and not to love is slavery.   To desire the word and not serve the
Lord may be possible; but to serve the Lord
and not desire his word is incredible.   If we
would relish the word of the Lord we must
engage in the work of the Lord.   If we would
get spiritual strength we must not only eat
spiritual food, but we must do spiritual work.

Eating and exercising go together.   The
one is dependent upon the other.   Exercise
is just as necessary to eating as air is to breath-
ing. If we eat carefully and exercise properly
we will live healthfully.   To eat much and
do nothing is laziness; to do much and eat
nothing is foolishness.   If we eat regularly
and exercise properly we will get strong physically.   But what shall we say pertaining to
spiritual eating and exercising?   Shall we
read much and do little?   Spiritually reading

and doing are just as important as eating and exercising. Eating furnishes the nutriment but exercise assimilates it; reading furnishes a supplement but we must make use of it. If we eat much food continually, it will lay heavily. Unless we exercise regularly we will feel miserably.

There is no assimilating without digesting; there is no digesting without exercising. If we would assimilate, believe what we read, we must thoroughly digest it. If we would thoroughly digest it we must use it; how can we use what we read unless we put it into practice? It is not only the knowing but the doing that makes us strong. We may know ever so much, but if we do ever so little, we will still be ever so weak. What good will our knowledge do us if we do not use it? It may be a source of gratification to us but it will never be the means of salvation to another.

THE RESULT OF SLOTH

But there is danger of eating too much and not exercising enough. So spiritually there is danger of reading too much and not doing enough. Those who eat a great deal and do very little are often taken with a severe case of the gout. You will pardon the expression, but are there not a great many Christians who have a bad case of the spiritual gout? They do not do enough to digest or assimilate what they read. They do not even exercise enough to limber up their joints. How many of them go on crutches and how slowly they get around. "Elbow-grease, like every other lubricator, will gum if not constantly used." Eating so much and doing so little explains the weakness of so many of us professing Christians.

How many of us are going about saying, "Oh, my weakness, my weakness!" It isn't our weakness, it is our laziness. A lazy person is always weak. We find fault with everything and are not able to do anything; we complain much and do little. If we are to do something then we cannot; even if we could we would not. It is not so much the "cannot" as the "will not." Our inability is often due to our inactivity. If we only did a little we would soon be able to do more. So long as we attempt nothing so long we will not be able to do much of anything. If we fully realize the consequences of doing nothing, and the blessing of doing something, then we would attempt great things. If we would do more we would complain less.

Spiritually, few of us suffer from doing too much; but, alas, how many of us suffer from doing too little! If we would suffer half as much from doing something as we do from doing nothing, then we would soon not suffer anything. If many of us would put forth as much effort in serving the Lord as we do in complaining of his word, then there would soon be no time for complaining at all. The only prescription for doing nothing is to do something. But how shall we do something when we do not feel able to do anything? Not doing anything when we can, that is indifference; desiring to do something when we cannot would at least be willingness. Of the former there are many; of the latter there are few. There will be two classes at the day of judgment: Those who did and those who did not. Some will say, "Lord, I would, but I could not;" but the Lord will say, "Nay, ye could, but ye would not." Oh! may it be said of us as it was said of the woman who anointed the Saviour's feet with precious ointment, and wiped them with her hair, "She hath done what she could;" or as the poor widow who cast in her two mites, "She hath done more than they all."

OVERWORK

Then there is not only danger of eating too much and not doing enough; but there is also danger of working too hard and not eating enough. To eat too much and not work. enough is either due to greediness or laziness; to work too much and not eat enough is either due to carelessness or stinginess. We ought not to work much without eating, any more than we ought to eat much without working. As we cannot expect to remain well long, if we eat too much without working; so we cannot expect to hold out long, if we work too much without eating.

It is the same spiritually. Often we do too much Christian work and do not eat enough spiritual food. We may do too much and not read enough. As it is disastrous to do too much physical work without eating, so it is perilous to do too much spiritual work without reading. As it is very easy to overeat without working so it is very easy to overwork without eating. If we were to eat too much and not do anything, our physical health would soon be gone. If we do too much and not read anything our spiritual strength will soon be overdone. As it would be dangerous to do six months' work without eating, so it would be perilous to do six months' Christian work without reading.

How often have you seen persons starting out on a Christian life and going to work as if they were determined to convert the world in six months; but in about six months their zeal was all gone, and it seems as if it would take the whole world to reconvert them. What was the matter? Why, they did too much spiritual work, and did not eat enough spiritual food. No! I will not say that they did too much spiritual work, but I will say that they did not eat enough spiritual food. Perhaps they should not have done less, but certainly they should have eaten more.

Constant working will require constant eating; but constant eating will also require constant working. If we work hard and eat nothing we will soon be despairing; so spiritually if we work hard and read nothing our strength will soon be wasting. Usually the more we work the more we eat; so spiritually the more we do the more we read. If you eat too much and do too little there is danger of indigestion; if you work too hard and eat too little there is danger of starvation.

THE EXERCISE OF FAITH

It is by exercise that we increase the strength that we already have. If I have strength and do not use it, it will not be long until I will lose it. The fish in the Mammoth cave have no eyes because there is no opportunity to use them; what, then, is the advantage to have them? So it is with our strength; if we do not use it we will not long have it. The servant that had one talent and hid it away, from him it was soon taken away. But the one that used his talents, to him were given still other talents. "For to him that hath shall be given, and from him that hath not shall be taken away even that which he hath." Not using our strength will be just as detrimental as abusing it; in both cases we are sure of losing it.

You remember the poor woman, in the days of Elisha, who had debts, but nothing with which to pay them; and the creditors came to take the two sons as security; but she cried to the prophet for help, and he said to her, "What hast thou in the house?" and she said, "Nothing but a pot of oil." He said: "Go to thy neighbors and borrow vessels, borrow not a few." Some of us would have said, "What for, Lord? I have nothing to put into them!"

But she believed the prophet, and went and borrowed the vessels. When she had procured the vessels, he said to her, "Take what little oil thou hast and pour it into the vessels." Oh, what faith this required!—pouring out what little oil she had, and the only thing she had in the house. We would have wanted to save what little we had, and have the prophet give us more. But no! "The Lord's ways are not our ways." We must use what we have in order to get more. Before this woman received more oil she had to lose what she had. So she began to pour out, and kept pouring until the vessels were full; and the oil stayed. Why should it not? The Lord does not waste anything. He blessed her just as much as she had capacity for being blessed. So it is with us; the Lord will only bless us to the extent of our capacity. He gives us no more strength than we can use. But even to get that blessing we do our part, we must use what we have.

Now you remember that prophet asked her, "What hast thou in the house?" He was going to have her use just what she had. I suppose if she had had flour he would have had her use that; if it would have been wood, I presume he would have had her use

that. He was going to have her use what she
had; she could not use what she did not have.
So it is with our strength; we are to use what
we have before we can have more. If we ever
get more strength we must use what we have.
The Lord deals with us and our strength as
he dealt with this woman and her oil. He
does not squander anything. He wastes not
strength upon us, by giving more than we can
use to us. Why should he give us more
strength when we do not use what we already
have? That would be wasting it. Use what
you have, and then you will soon have more
to use.

GAIN BY LOSS

But you say, "I must save my strength; it
will not do to use it." The way to save your
strength is to lose it. The farmer who sows
his seed must for a time lose it. If he did not
sow he would not reap. The Egyptian throwing his seed upon the receding waters of the
Nile, to one who did not know their method
of sowing, would seem like entirely wasting
it; but in a short time where the waters had
been, will be seen fruitful fields and golden
harvests as the result of it. He lost the little
seed that he had, cheerfully, in order that he

might reap more bountifully. Would we have more strength then we must use the little strength that we now have. If this woman would not have used the little oil that she had, it would have been but a short time until she would have had none to use. But she used what little she had and she received all that she was prepared to receive. We may need all the strength that we have, but if we will use it, we will soon have all that we need.

But you say, "I haven't any strength." I think you have. Paul said, "When I am weak then am I strong." Consciousness of weakness, often is the corner-stone of strength. Often when we feel the weakest then we are the strongest. A plea of weakness is often but an excuse for unwillingness.

The Lord has given every man some spiritual strength; every man has a religious nature. The most degraded heathen have some religious proclivity; then are we going to say that we have no spiritual capacity? We have had it, but may have lost it by not using it. There are many of us who now have no spiritual strength, simply because we did not use what we once had. "We have labored in vain; we have spent our strength for naught." But why do we think that we have no spiritual strength? If we once put to the test what we have, we might have more than we think. To think that we have no strength, often is simply an excuse for not using what we have. We might be surprised at the strength we really possessed when we once put it to a thorough test.

FAITH UNTRAMMELED

You remember the palsied man, do you not? Did he have much strength? Why, no! At least he thought he hàd not; it took four men to carry him about; they brought him to the Lord and let him down through the roof to get him where the Saviour was. When the Lord saw him he said to him, "Take up thy bed and walk." The man did not say, "Why, Lord, how can I? I have no strength; I have not moved a muscle for a long time, and how do you expect me to get up and walk?" But he did not talk after this fashion. When the Lord told him to take up his bed and walk he believed that he had strength; and he put forth one mighty effort, and got up and walked forth with his couch. No doubt he was surprised at his strength; he was not aware of it until he had thoroughly tested it. Neither can we tell how much strength we have until we put forth an effort to use it. When Christ gave the command, with it he also gave the power to do it. But how shall we know of that power if we do not obey the command? If the man would not have put forth the effort to test his strength he no doubt ever after would have doubted whether he had any strength. He no doubt would have thought that it was a rash command and that it would have been vain to obey such a command.

But, my reader, how often has the Lord commanded us in his word to arise and we felt as though we had no strength and did not believe his word. The Lord has commanded but we have not obeyed, and his word has been doubted. How often have we made out the Lord as untruthful, because we have been so unfaithful. How often have we deemed the obeying of his command impossible; but it is not the impossibility, nor inability, but our infidelity. God does not require of us anything impossible. It may seem impossible for us, but all things are possible with God. If we are on the Lord's side the Lord will be on our side, and all things will be possible for us. Putting our strength against His will not diminish His any, but it will hinder ours much; letting our strength fall right in with His will not increase His any, but will help ours much. This palsied man had not much strength, but when he threw what he had in with the Lord's it helped him to accomplish what he thought was impossible to accomplish. There is such a thing as using our strength against God and losing it, then there is such a thing as losing our strength in God and saving it.

To have no physical strength is a great misfortune; to say that we have no spiritual strength may be a great delusion. We might have physical strength if we had not abused what we once had.

To have no physical strength may be caused by gross neglect; to have no spiritual strength will be the cause of eternal regret. It is bad enough to be a physical invalid temporally, but what must it be to be a spiritual invalid eternally? The former is the consequence of physical laws temporally transgressed; the second is the transgression of spiritual laws eternally punished. If we would be strong eternally then we must begin to grow in strength spiritually; but spiritually we cannot be strong eternally, unless we use the spiritual strength we have temporally. If we use the spiritual strength that we have in time, we will not have much weakness to regret in eternity.

WHEN, WHERE, AND HOW?

But *when* and *where* and *how* shall we use our strength? Use it whenever, wherever and however we can use it the best.

Whenever? Now. "Say not ye there are still four months and then cometh the harvest? Behold, I say unto you, lift up your eyes and look on the fields; for they are white already to harvest."

Oh, that we would but see the fields of ripening grain, then might we also see the need of saving perishing men!

Do we know the danger of deferring the harvest longer? When the harvest is ripe, then it is time for reaping it; if we do not we may be sure of losing it. When the grain is ripe and we do not reap it, then the wind will blow and soon shatter it. We are deferring the harvest at a great cost, and if we do not reap it, it will be lost. As wheat may get too ripe for reaping so may men be left until they are past saving. Our procrastination may be the cause of their eternal condemnation. There is an opportune time in the life of every man when he might be garnered into the kingdom of heaven; if he is not, it may be a wrong which we have committed, that may never be forgiven; drifting over that time he is invariably lost, and if he is my brother, who is to blame the most? There are times when men are convicted, when by a little effort on our part, they might be converted; but let them drift past conviction, there would be but little hope of their conversion. There are many souls that might be saved to-day, which may be lost to-morrow. The field that ought to be reaped to-day, may have to be gleaned to-morrow. The sheaf that is too ripe for reaping, is like the soul that has been neglected too long for saving. Yes, my brother, lift up your eyes and see the fields already white for the harvest. Will you say, "No; it is four months yet, then is the harvest?" Till then many precious sheaves may be scattered and lost. There are many that might be saved, shall we put forth the effort to save them? If we do not we must glean what we can after Satan has ruined them. Oh, let us put forth our sickles to reap the precious grain; let us put forth our strength to save perishing men. If we are to save them we must at once garner them; if we do not at once garner them we will soon lose them. It is far better to save them, at almost any cost, than to neglect them and have them lost.

"And he that reapeth receiveth wages and gathereth fruit to life eternal." "They that be wise shall shine as the firmament, and they that turn many to righteousness as the stars forever and ever." "Let him know that he who converteth a sinner from the error of his way, shall save a soul from death and hide a multitude of sins." Shall not this lead every one of us to immediate action? What then shall constrain us? If the hope of eternal remuneration for ourselves will not, then will the damnation of others? If the eternal joy of a soul saved will not do it, then neither will the awful condition of a soul lost do it. If the field of golden grain will not invite us to its reaping, much less will the awful condition of a shattered harvest incite us to its gleaning. If we care not whether we ourselves are crowned, we care little if another is damned. If we care not for the glorious reward of ourselves, neither will we care for the terrible punishment of another. But shall not the blessedness of another soul saved, and the double blessedness of our own crown, move us to immediate action?

WHERE SHALL WE USE OUR STRENGTH?

Then *where* shall we use it? Wherever we can; and we can wherever we are. Few are ever placed under circumstances where there are no opportunities for doing good. All of us could do some good if we were only constrained so that we would. To be where you can see no need of doing good must certainly be spiritual blindness; not to hear the call where you can do good must certainly be spiritual deafness. "No one is so blind as the man that will not see; no one so deaf as the man who will not hear." To be where you see the need of doing good and then not doing it, must be cold indifference; to hear the call and then not respond to it must be hard-heartedness. He that does the best he can in the place where he is, will soon have a better place than where he is. He who is bent on doing good will go where he can do the most good. If we all did the best we could we might then defy Satan to do what he would; if we did our best we might then defy him to do his worst. But so long as we are indifferent, so long he will not be recreant; while we are doubting he is recruiting. Oh, that every one only used his strength as best he knew, we would not need to fear Satan for the worst he could do. There are many of us who may not take a stand for lack of boldness; but there are far more who will not do it because of their spiritual coldness.

SPIRITUAL EXERCISES

Now there is a spiritual exercise in which everyone may engage. It will strengthen those who partake in it. It is witnessing for Christ wherever you are. Everyone has this talent, for we are using it every day for some-one. "Whose witnesses are ye?" We say we cannot witness; and yet we do. We are tes-tifying for someone or for something, by word or deed; by life and action; by our look and conversation. Now those of us who have con-fessed Christ, "Shall we not also so walk, even as he walked?" If we possess him shall we not also confess him? If we have accepted him shall we not also witness for him? To confess him and not possess him would be hypocrisy; to possess him and not confess him would be almost an impossibility.

Christ said to his disciples, "Ye shall be wit-nesses unto me;" but where? "First in Jeru-salem, then in Judea and Samaria, and then to the uttermost parts of the earth." First they were to be witnesses in Jerusalem, this

is where they were; then in all Judea, which
was all around them; then in Samaria, which
was next available for them. And then? "To
the uttermost parts of the earth." What an
example of usefulness! If we do the best we
can where we are, then there will soon be
larger circles of usefulness for us. If we are
faithful in Jerusalem we will soon have opportunity to go into all Judea; and when we have
done what we can there then we can have
Samaria; when we have done our best in
Samaria then we can have the uttermost parts
of the earth.

But what may we learn? If we do not do
our best in Jerusalem, we will not have an
opportunity to do anything in Judea; if we
do not do our best in Judea we can never do
much in Samaria. If we have witnessed in
Jerusalem and Judea and Samaria, then will
we be able to go as witnesses to the uttermost
parts of the earth. Often we hear men talk
about going as missionaries to foreign fields;
what have they ever done in their own fields?
How can we expect them to do much abroad
when they have never done much at home?
Why do they talk about saving souls in China,
in Japan, in India and Africa, when they have
never said a word to those whose souls are

perishing at their next door? Why do they
talk of saving the Chinaman in a foreign field
when they have never said a word to the
Chinaman in their home field? The disciples
were not to witness in Judea until they had
witnessed in Jerusalem. The Lord has never
called persons to a foreign land until they
have done the best they could in their own'
land. Missionary boards may have sent them,
but did the Lord call them? The Lord calls
the man who does the best he can. We do
not know who will do much; then shall we
send him forth who has done nothing? The
Lord sometimes chooses men from what He
knows they will do, but we must choose them
from what they have done; because we cannot know what they will do. But this we
know, that if they have done much in Jerusalem, then they will also do something in
Judea; if they have done what they could
where they were, then we well may rest as-
sured that they will do something wherever
they are. There are men who have done little abroad who did much at home; but there
are few who have done much abroad who
have done little at home. Shall we give to
the man ten talents who did not use the one?
The Lord would not do it. It would not be

economy. If we do the best we can in our own sphere we will soon have a larger sphere. "For he that is faithful over a few things I will make him ruler over many things." But you say, Where is my place of work; where am I to use my strength? Well, organized effort is always the best, and if we can throw our strength in with such an effort it will tell the most. In this day of Christian organization there certainly should be no lack of place for such effort. The church with her division of labor will furnish opportunity for all who wish to work in the service of the Lord. The Young People's Society of Christian Endeavor; the Sunday schools; the Young Men's Christian Associations, will surely furnish us all the work that we might desire to do. There is a place for everyone, and everyone ought to be in his place. If we do not seek after it, then it is very evident that we are not very anxious for it; if we really desire a place we will find it, but if we would find it we must also work for it. To desire a place and not seek it would be insincerity; to find it and then not fill it would belie our integrity. Whenever the church is not large enough for our field of labor, *then* the Lord will send us to labor in a larger field. Let us find our place and fill it, then we will soon have a larger place to fill. "Let us not be a square peg in a round hole." Let us fit into some place where we can do much good, then the place will soon fit us where we can do more good. There are many places that need us. The church needs us, the world needs us. Let us do all we can in our church, then we can do more in the world. What the world needs at this present time is not men to fill the best places, but men who will fill their places best. We do not need more men so much as we need some who are more men. There may be men plenty enough, but what we want are men that are good enough. There are men of many kinds, but what we need are more men of a better kind. Gideon's army increased was not worth as much as Gideon's army diminished. We do not need better places for men, but we need better men for places.

STRENGTH FOR PERSONAL WORK

Then *how* shall we do it? By personal work; by every person working with one other person. "Hand-picked fruit is the best." The farmer who gathers his apples that he may keep them over winter does not club the tree or shake the limbs so that they fall to the ground, but he climbs the tree and picks them one by one, carefully handling them so that they shall not be bruised. Oh, that we might so save souls, one at a time, and caring for them so that they might be carefully kept for eternity!

Personal work is not the most efficient way to strengthen ourselves only, but it is the most efficient way to redeem others also. It is not only the best kind of a gymnasium for ourselves, but it is also the best means of salvation for others. There is nothing that so strengthens us as when we put forth our strength to save others. But which is the more important, to strengthen ourselves or save others? What is the difference, when in doing the latter we do the former? If in saving others we strengthen ourselves, then it is more important to save others. If, then, personal work is the method that will be doubly beneficial, why not use it? If it is the most effective, why not adopt it? Satan understands this method and he uses it to good advantage. He sees no advantage in using another method. His work is hand-to-hand work. Personal influence, personal effort, is what he uses. Our young men that are going into the paths of woe, have they been led astray in mass meetings held by the servants of Satan? No. He never holds any such meetings. Have any of our young men ever been persuaded by a strong appeal of one of Satan's servants to take sides with them? No! He makes no such appeals. They have been led astray by the hand, and through the personal influence of one of the servants of Satan. Some one person associating with some other person has led him astray. Though it may have been done unintentionally, yet it has been done most effectively. Satan does not ruin many at a time; he does it one at a time. His efforts are personal, *but they are effectual.* Have you ever known Satan to have large meetings and then enlisting men in his service by eloquently telling them the fruits of his service? No! But what does he do? He says to this servant of his, "Go influence that man;" he says to that one, "Go make him your associate until you have ruined him." Thus every servant of Satan is at work personally to ruin some other person. This is his method. It is the best method. It is not the best method because it is his method, but it is his method because it is the best method. It seems as if the best method has been put

to the worst use, but have we not been trying
to put the poorest method to the best use?
Can it be true that "the children of this world
are wiser in their generation than the children
of light?" Can it be true that Satan is using
a method successfully to ruin men, while we
are adopting it reluctantly to save them?

THE SERVICE OF SATAN

But why is it that the servants of Satan
serve him so faithfully? Because he gives them
something to do personally. He is binding
them to him by binding them to someone else.
The more they serve him the more they are
bound to him. But what shall be the hope
of getting servants for the Lord? By constantly having men serve the Lord. They
who constantly serve Satan will sooner or
later be enslaved by Satan, but those who
constantly serve the Lord will sooner or later
be strong in the Lord. The more we serve
the Lord the better we will love the Lord.
The service of Satan, though at first it may be
joy, in the end will be slavery; but the service of the Lord, though at first it may seem
like slavery, yet in the end it will be joy.
Some think that the service that we give to
the Lord is spent for naught; then the serv-

ice that we give to Satan is spent for far worse than naught. Though the former to some may not be a plus quantity, the latter to all must be a minus quantity. "The path of the just is as a shining light which shineth brighter and brighter unto the perfect day." But how shall it be with the wicked? "Wherefore their way shall be unto them as slippery ways in darkness. They shall be driven on and fall therein."

THE SERVICE OF THE WORLD

But personal work is also the method of business. How do men sell their goods? Do they wait until they have a sufficient audience so that they can sell to them at auction? No! They sell to them one at a time; and the fewer people around the more liable they are to sell their goods. Men sell at auction when they expect to go out of business. Are we as stewards of the Lord's work thinking of going out of business? No! Then we had better adopt that method which will insure us more success in that business. If we do not make a business of our religion we will not long have a religion to make a business of. Why should men's business be conducted on more successful principles than the Lord's business? If men succeed better in their business by personal work, why then should we hesitate to do the Lord's business by personal work?

TnE LORD'S METHOD

Was not the method of the Lord that of personal work? While He spoke to multitudes He dealt with the individual; while He went about doing good all the time, He did it principally to one at a time. His life-work was personal work. He did not heal many at a time but He healed one at a time. He did not say to the blind man, who cried, "Lord, have mercy on me," "Come up to Jerusalem where I am waiting for a sufficient number to justify my healing, and just as soon as there is a sufficient number I will heal you." He had no such method, He said no such a thing; He healed him right then and there. Think of Him dealing with the woman at the well to have her accept eternal life. Did He tell her that He was pastor of a church in the city and that He hoped she would attend His church and be converted? No! He did all he could to have her converted right then and there.

THE DISCIPLES' WORK

The disciples of the Lord did most of their

work by personal work. Though they were sent out two by two, they dealt with persons one by one. When Andrew found the Lord he went straightway and brought Simon his brother to Him. If we go after men in person we will be more likely to get the person we go after. It is more important to have one man start out and hold out than to have a hundred start out and then give out. We might persuade multitudes and have them confess Christ; but it is better to have one man and not let him go until he possess Christ. To take one person and develop him, that is commendable; but to undertake one hundred men and then let go of them, that is lamentable.

Look at Philip: He was down there at Samaria preaching Christ to the people, and many were saved; but right in the midst of this great work, the angel of the Lord spake unto him saying, "Arise, go toward the south, unto the way that goeth down from Jerusalem unto Gaza, *which is desert.*" Here is a servant of the Lord preaching Christ unto many who were giving heed to his words, but right there in the midst of it there comes the command, "Philip, arise and go down toward Gaza, which is desert." Why, what did he want Philip to go down in the desert for? Who was down there to convert? Philip might have said, "I cannot go down there into the desert because it is beneath my dignity;" but Philip thought less of his dignity than he did of his duty. He might have thought, Am I not doing a great work here and why should I go down there?" I presume he was saving ten souls in Samaria for one that he would save in the desert. Most of us would have said, "I do not believe that I am called to go down there in the desert to preach while I am doing so great a work here in Samaria; I must have mistaken the call." Philip did not talk thus; but what did he do? *Why, he arose and went!*

But as he was going down through the desert toward Gaza, what happened? "Behold a man of Ethiopia, a eunuch of great authority under Candace, queen of the Ethiopians, who had the charge of all her treasure, was returning; and sitting in his chariot read Isaiah the prophet." Ah! Can we not now see why the Lord commanded Philip to go down into the desert? There was a rare fish to be caught indeed—a prince to be converted.

THE WORTH OF A SOUL

But why was it so important to save a prince? Was his soul worth more than any other man's soul? No! His soul was not worth more, but the saving of it might amount to more. In the lives of some, there are wrapt up far greater possibilities than in other lives. The conversion of this prince might have been worth more in possibilities than the conversion of all Samaria. Think of the influence he would have over his people! It is often more probable for a prince to convert his whole kingdom than for a whole kingdom to convert its prince. May not the conversion of this prince mean the Christianizing of another kingdom? The Lord, who sees the end from the beginning, saw great possibilities in the conversion of this man, so He had Philip leave his great work and go down there into the desert and convert him.

Notice the fortunate concurrence of events: The Lord knew that this prince was to go along about such a time, and so He had Philip to be there at that time. What would have been the result if Philip would have been ten minutes late? Why, he would have missed the eunuch, and his journey would have been for naught. Then Philip might have blamed the Lord for having made a mistake in calling him down there. Nevertheless the Lord would have been blameless, but Philip would have been without excuse; for the Lord knew the eunuch's time in passing, but Philip would have missed it on account of his tardiness in going; but Philip obeyed, and he arrived in time to see the eunuch pass by.

THE PROMPTING OF THE SPIRIT

I imagine, as Philip saw the prince passing by, he said to himself, "Ah! I see now why the Lord wanted me down here in the desert! There is a prince to be converted;" and while he was thus thinking the spirit said, "Philip, go near and join thyself to this chariot." Did Philip mistake the promptings of the spirit? No! *He ran thither to him.* He did not begin to say to himself, "Oh, it is not worth while to speak to that man; why, he is a prince, riding along in a fine chariot, and I am walking through the desert; he will not listen to me; I might insult him if I speak to him; it is a great offense to speak to a prince without being requested." He did not do this. When the spirit prompted him he did not walk slowly, hoping that the prince would pass so that he would have an excuse for not talking to him; but when the spirit prompted him he ran thither to him. And as he came near he saw that he was reading Isaiah the prophet: and Philip said to him, "Understandest thou what thou readest?"

Think of that! A man down there in the desert, without any ceremony running up to a man and getting into his chariot and asking him whether he knew what he was reading about. But ah! Philip was constrained; he thought not of the intrusion to the man, but all about the conversion of the man. He would rather make a mistake in an effort to save him than to have him lost without any effort to save him. He forgot the danger in his great earnestness to save the man. So he just ran thither and joined himself to this chariot, knowing that if the Lord commanded it, that he also had arranged for it.

But, my brother, how often has the spirit said to you as you were walking along the streets, "There goes one to whom you ought to speak in regard to his eternal welfare;" but instead of running to him and opening the subject, you have walked slower, hoping that he might have passed before you got near him; so that you might have an excuse for not speaking to him. Oh, how often have we neglected the promptings of the spirit! Have we not had as distinct a command to speak to our comrades, as Philip had to speak to this Ethiopian? Yes! But we did not know it. But Philip obeyed and was strengthened; we disobeyed and were weakened.

When Philip asked the eunuch whether he understood what he was reading, what did the eunuch say? Did he become angry because of the intrusion? No! He afterward rejoiced in his conversion. The Lord evidently had opened the way for Philip, and nothing could delay or hinder him. He must have touched the eunuch's heart or Philip never would have found the way to it.

AN OPPORTUNITY SEIZED

When Philip asked him the question, "Understandest thou what thou readest?" he said, "How can I understand unless someone guide me?" Then Philip opened his mouth and *"preached unto him Jesus."* Yes, not some theory of his own; not some historical research of prophecy; not some philosophical interpretation of theology; *but he preached unto him Jesus.* What would have been the result if he had begun to talk to him about the condition of politics or the signs of the times?

He never would have been converted. Philip might have conversed with him about the affairs in his dominions. But no! He was too much concerned about his salvation. Philip knew that this was his opportunity, and that this was why the Lord had sent him into the desert; and he did not like to return until he saw the prince converted.

Do you not think that Philip was strengthened after he was thus tried? Do you think that he ever would have doubted, after he was thus tested? The reason many of us are not stronger in the Lord is because we do not obey the voice of the Lord. If Philip had not obeyed, the eunuch would have remained unconverted; and in Philip's mind, God would not have been vindicated. Through the obedience of Philip the prince was converted. He came reading about Christ; he went rejoicing in Christ. If we want to do great things we must begin by doing little things. If we want to save multitudes then we must begin by saving individuals. We will never save many at a time until we begin saving one at a time. The best way to learn to do public work is to begin doing personal work. It might be better to preach in the desert to one than to preach in Samaria to many. It is often not as well

to do a little good to many at a time, as it is
to do much good to one at a time.

STRENGTH FOR ALL

And now we may have strength if we desire
it. It will, however, take proper reading
and constant doing to acquire it. Shall we be
excused whose strength has been abused?
No! We shall be wanting whose spiritual
strength has been failing. In the day of
judgment many of us will say that we could
not withstand the evil because of our weakness. Nay! We had better say that we
would not on account of our laziness. He
who hath strength and uses it not, will want
to use it in a day when he hath it not. Our
spiritual inability is more often occasioned by
our negligence than by God's providence.
Our carelessness is the cause often of our
spiritual weakness. If God would have given
us our spirits without anything to feed them,
then we might be acquitted, but when we
might sit down to a feast at his word and will
not, it is to be very much regretted. "Verily,
verily, none of these shall eat of my supper."
If we will not accept an invitation to his feast
on earth, shall we then sit down to his feast
in heaven? If we neglect the spiritual food

here we will not taste of the heavenly food there. What we will enjoy in heaven will depend much upon what we have enjoyed on earth. Spiritually there is no such a thing as being a pauper here and a prince in heaven. We who have starved our souls here, how can we expect to be filled there? We who have eaten the meat of Satan's providing, must eternally eat the crumbs of our own deserving. We who have sipped the cup of our own liking, must finally drink the dregs of our own choosing.

If our Father had not set before us something better, then He might be blamable, but as long as we shall not want, so long we are inexcusable. He shall supply all our needs; why then should we want? Because we often want what we do not need.

GROWTH IN SERVICE

It is by reading that we know, but it is by doing that we grow. It were better to know little and do much, than to know much and do little. Our judgment will not be on the ground of knowing but on the ground of doing; not from the strength that we have had, but from what we have used. The final test will not be what have you known, but what have you done.   It will not be, "as much as ye have known," but, "as often as ye have done." Most of us know better than we do, but how few of us do better than we know.   The man who does better than he knows will fare better than the man who knows better than he does.   "He that knoweth to do good and doeth it not to him it is sin."   The awful judgment will not be on the ground of not knowing but on the ground of not doing.   It is said of our Master that "He began to do and to teach."   Alas!   How many of us are trying to teach and not to do.   We would not have men know less, but, oh! if they only *did* more! To have two talents and use them is better than to have ten talents and lose them.   If the man who had one talent, and did not use it, was called unprofitable, then we who have ten talents and have not used them must certainly be unpardonable.   It is well enough to know but it is far better to do.   "For it is written: If ye know these things, happy are ye if ye do them."

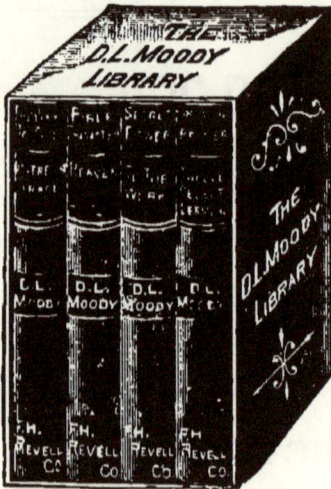